Food in Colonial America

By Mark Thomas

Welcome Books

Children's Press®
A Division of Scholastic Inc.
New York / Toronto / London / Auckland / Sydney
Mexico City / New Delhi / Hong Kong
Danbury, Connecticut

Photo Credits: Cover, pp. 5, 7, 9, 11, 19 © Colonial Williamsburg Foundation;
p. 13 © Hulton/Archive by Getty Image; p. 15 © Mark E. Gibson/Corbis (2 men),
Corbis Visions of Nature Royalty free CD (background); p. 17 © Richard T. Nowitz/Corbis
Contributing Editor: Jennifer Silate
Book Design: Erica Clendening

Library of Congress Cataloging-in-Publication Data

Thomas, Mark, 1963–
    Food in Colonial America / by Mark Thomas.
        p. cm. — (Colonial America)
    Includes index.
    Summary: Simple text and photographs depict some foods and cooking techniques of
    American colonists.
    ISBN 0-516-23936-8 (lib. bdg.) — ISBN 0-516-23491-9 (pbk.)
    1. Cookery, American—History—17th century—Juvenile literature. 2. Cookery, American—
History—18th century—Juvenile literature. 3. United States—History—Colonial period, ca.
1600–1775—Juvenile literature. [1. Cookery, American—History—17th century. 2. Cookery,
American—History—18th century. 3. United States—History—Colonial period, ca. 1600–1775.]
I. Title. II. Colonial America (Children's Press)

TX715 .T425 2002
394.1'0973'09032—dc21

                                                    2001042471

Contents

Most people in **Colonial America** grew much of their food.

They grew **grains**, fruits, and vegetables to eat.

5

Corn was an important grain for people in Colonial America.

Colonists made many different foods with corn.

7

Colonists made bread from the grains they grew.

Bread took a long time to make.

Farmers often had cows on their farms.

They got milk from the cows.

11

Colonists made butter from the milk.

They used a **churn** to make the butter.

13

Many colonists had to **hunt** for food, too.

They hunted fish, turkey, deer, and many other animals.

Mostly men and boys hunted.

15

Women did most of the cooking in Colonial America.

16

17

Colonists had to cook their food in a **fireplace**.

They did not have ovens like we do today.

19

People in Colonial America worked hard to grow, hunt, and cook their own food.

21

New Words

churn (**chern**) a container in which milk is
beaten and shaken to make butter

Colonial America (kuh-**loh**-nee-uhl uh-**mer**-
uh-kuh) the time before the United States
became a country (1620–1780)

colonists (**kahl**-uh-nihsts) people who leave
a country to live in a new place or colony

fireplace (**fyr**-plays) a stone or brick area
where it is safe to have a fire

grains (**graynz**) wheat, oats, corn, rice, and
other cereal grasses

hunt (**huhnt**) to catch wild animals to eat

To Find Out More

Books
Colonial Life
by Bobbie Kalman
Crabtree Publishing

Hasty Pudding, Johnnycakes, and Other Good Stuff: Cooking in Colonial America
by Loretta Frances Ichord
Millbrook Press

Web Site
Colonial Williamsburg Foundation History
http://history.org/history/index.html
Learn about Colonial American life on Colonial Williamsburg's official site.

Index

About the Author
Mark Thomas has written more than fifty children's and young adult books. He writes and teaches in Florida.

Reading Consultants
Kris Flynn, Coordinator, Small School District Literacy, The San Diego County Office of Education

Shelly Forys, Certified Reading Recovery Specialist, W.J. Zahnow Elementary School, Waterloo, IL

Sue McAdams, Former President of the North Texas Reading Council of the IRA, and Early Literacy Consultant, Dallas, TX